Inspired by Granny

Thanks for being an angel on earth, to my Bryan.

This book is dedicated to Bryan, Ann, and Clyde .

My heart is with you in your time of sorrow.
Wishing you peace and strength during
this difficult time.
May this book give you some comfort.

To my children,
thanks for being my little helpers, my motivation,
and my biggest supporters.
I could not have completed this book without you.

I love you to the moon and back!

I'LL BE THERE EVERY DAY, BUT IN A DIFFERENT KIND OF WAY !

Written by Marquita Goodluck
Illustrated by Theresa Stites

Every day it was always the same, we went to
see Granny, come sun or come rain.
Since Granny didn't live at home, we never wanted her to feel alone.
So, we would come filled with stories and soft kisses,
telling Granny about our day and our wishes.

ENID BARON
HOME FOR THE
ELDERLY

ENTER

MAIN
LOBBY

GRANNY

But this one day...

felt quite strange,

something was different,

something had changed.

I looked around

but could not see,

but then I noticed

there was no Granny.

I looked up to see my mother.
No one spoke, not even an utter.

Then my mother turned to say,
that our dear Granny has passed away.

As I began to shed a tear,

I felt them come

then disappear.

In that moment,
    I remembered a day
        when Granny had alot to say.

She told me to listen
to the words I share, because one day
    you will need them.

So I listened with care...

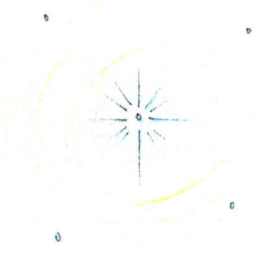

Listen, my child...

there will come a day
when I will have to go away.

But when I do, don't shed a tear
because remember my love,
I am always near.

I'll be there everyday,
but in a different kind of way.

You may say Granny
and my response you won't hear,
but never doubt it,
I am there.

Always remember, I am everywhere!

Every wind, every tree, every flower,

that's where I'll be!

For a while,
there will be sadness and pain.
Things will just not feel quite the same.
Always remember what I say,
I will be there everyday
in a
different kind of way!
Don't think of me as sick or sad,
my little one,
I will be quite glad!

I will be free to to do the things
you can't believe !

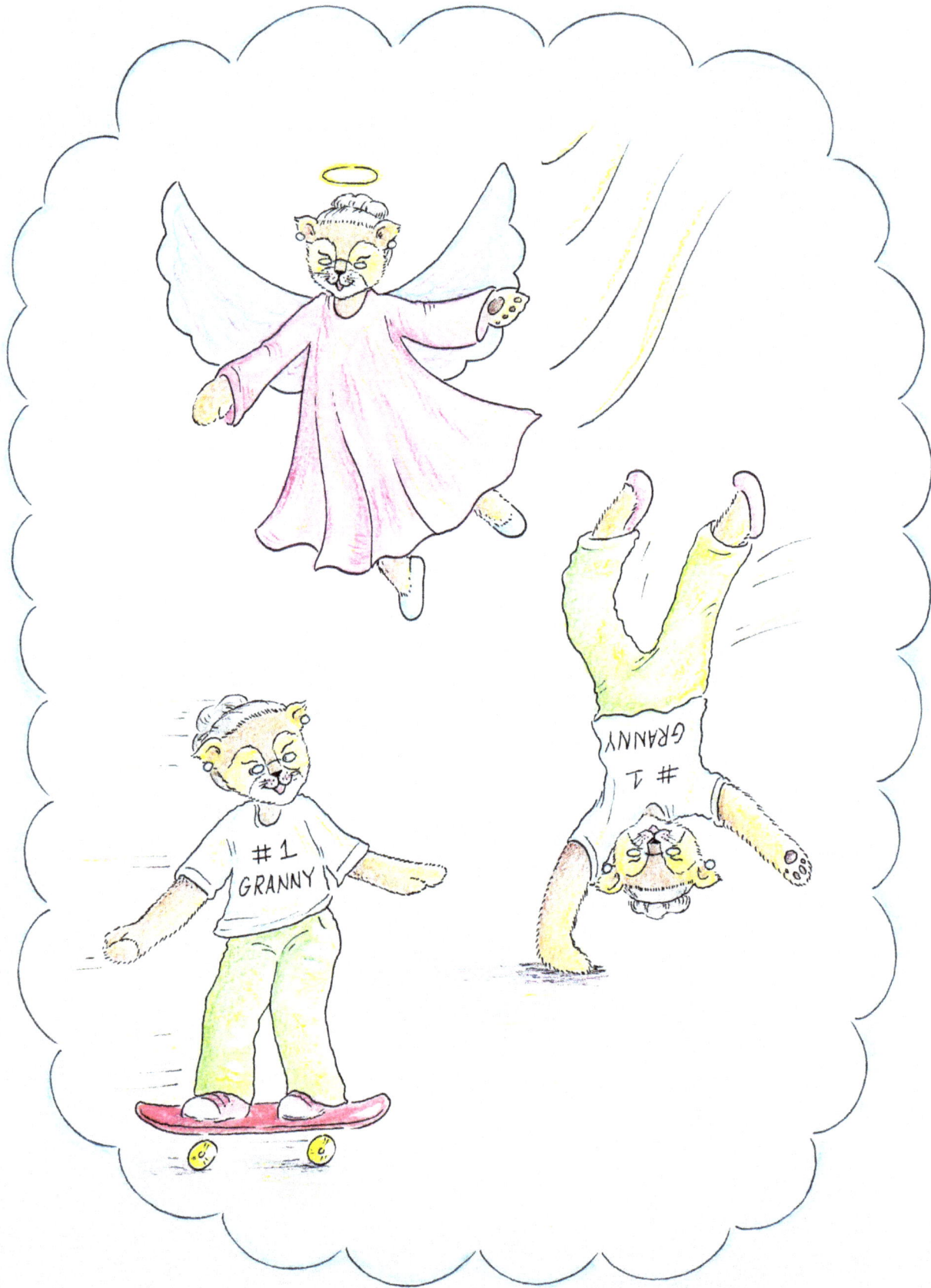

Inside each person
lies a spirit,

you can't feel it or hear it.
It is who you are inside,
it is where you show your pride.

When my days on Earth are over,
then my spirit will take over.

I will live in a special place

filled with love, happiness,

and

His Grace.

Have no fear about
where I am going.

It's a beautiful place worth showing.
I am one person.

There is so many of you.
I had to change to get a better view.

Now I can clearly see
what is expected of me.

Remember darling, I was lonely and sick,
my body could not handle it.

I begged to God to be released
and now all my pain has ceased.

We will never be closer than ever before,
no need to call or walk out the door.

Just speak to me wherever you are,
no matter how far.

Never will we be apart,
I will live within your heart!

At times you will be sad and mad,

but try to remember the fun times we had!

Our memories are our friend,

they will live forever and never end.

Remember darling, I was lonely and sick, my body could not handle it.
I begged to God to be released and now all my pain has ceased.
We will never be closer than ever before, no need to call or walk out the door.
Just speak to me wherever you are, no matter how far.
Never will we be apart, I will live within your heart!

I am always
with you

www.ingramcontent.com/pod-product-compliance
Lightning Source LLC
Chambersburg PA
CBHW062022090426
42811CB00005B/921